BABIES DON'T SUCK

For those who've found themselves upside down

BABIES DON'T SUCK

Aaron Blabey

MACMILLAN
Pan Macmillan Australia

 is for *Arrival*.

No, not the baby.

You.

You've arrived home to a life you no longer recognise.

DO NOT PANIC.

Get a beer,
follow the alphabet,
and everything will be cool.

So obviously, **B** is for *Baby*.

On the one hand,
the most beautiful thing you've ever seen.

On the other,
a tsunami wrapped in a blanket.

And that probably means C is for *Capsized*.

Because there's no way around it,
D is for
Deprivation.

But it is also for

DO NOT PANIC.

And here's why …

You see,  might well be for

Extremely Sore Nipples

(Not yours. Hers.)

BUT THEY
WON'T LAST FOREVER.

THINGS I'D LIKE TO STOP TALKING ABOUT

1. Lactation
2. Attachment
3. How often the baby produces turds
4. Organic carrots
5. Safety rails
6. High-school enrolment 13 years in advance
7. Cloth nappy guilt

25. Hemorrhoids

This will all

And sure, **F** is for

Fucking Car Seats,

port-a-cots, highchairs, prams, strollers and other

Freedom Annihilators

BUT you need to remember that these things are

TEMPORARY.

Of course, that can be hard to remember when

 is for *Grown-Up Stuff*,

which is all you seem to do now.

BUT …

… the good news is, H is for *Hope*.

And if you can hang on,
you just might find that life
can be **EVEN BETTER** than it was.

No, really.

You see, **I** is for **In The Trenches**, which is where you are now.

And **J** is for
Jumping Into The Unknown,
which is where you are heading.

But here's the thing …

K is for the *Kid*

who will one day need *you* just as much as they currently need their mum.

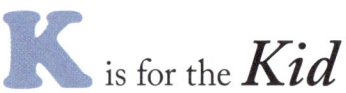

And they will **L**_iterally_ jump up and down squealing with joy at the idea of hanging out with you.

Which is not half bad.

That said, children also bring
Madness
with a capital
.

They are CHAOS.

Wild, shrieking, nut-busting chaos.

But do not despair.

Because **N** is for the *Nano-Second* it takes for that baby to turn into an actual person with opinions of their own.

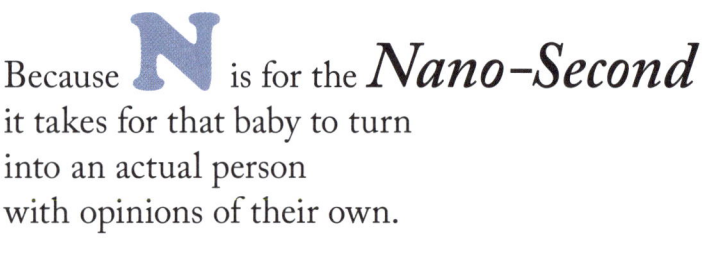

And then suddenly **O** is for
Oh Shit, Where'd Our Baby Go?
and

P is for the *Pang* you'll feel as you remove that car seat because they just don't need it anymore.

And, if you make **Q** for as many
Quiet Evenings Alone
with your girl as you can,

then **R** can be for a *Relationship*
that is happy and functioning despite the chaos.

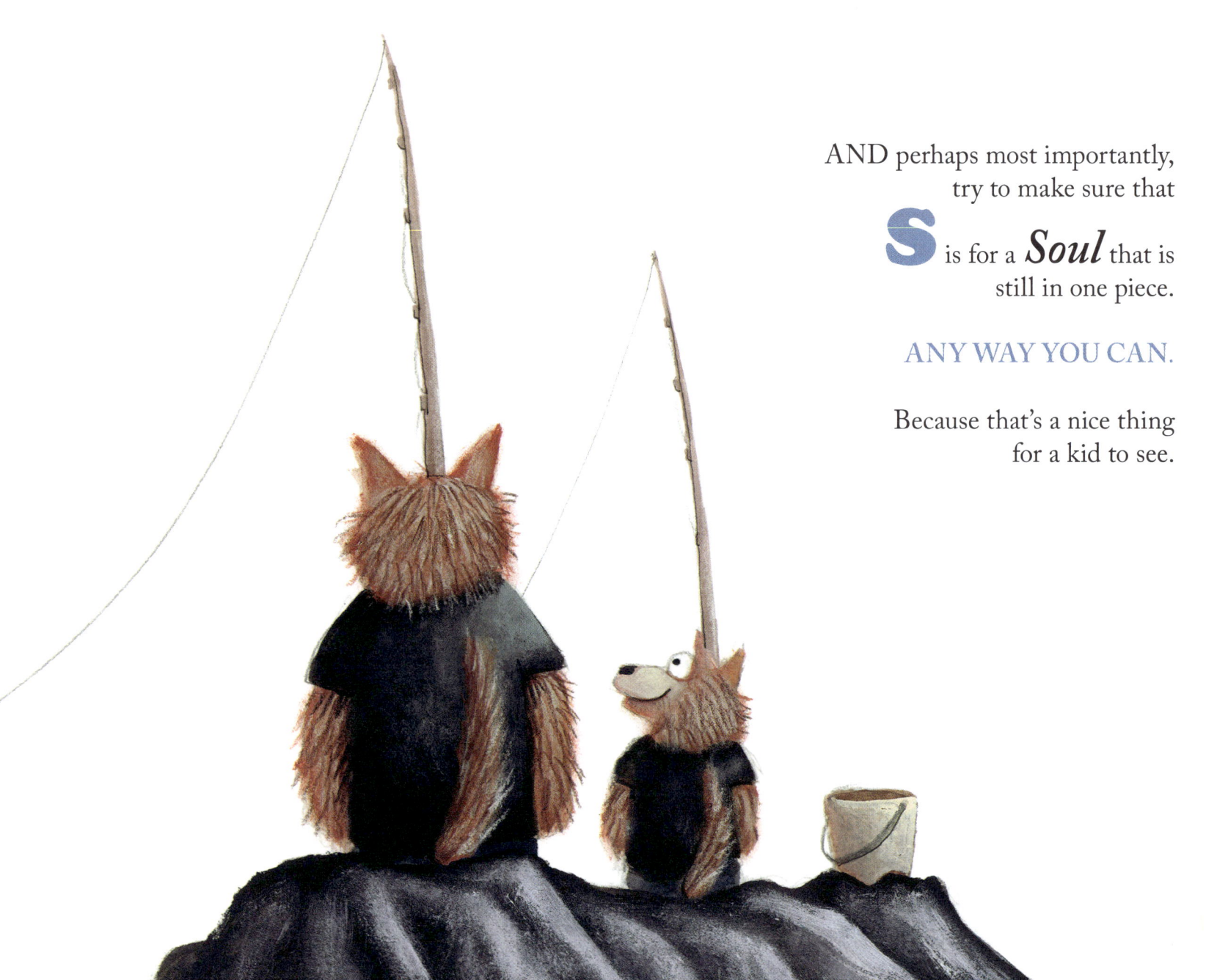

AND perhaps most importantly, try to make sure that

S is for a *Soul* that is still in one piece.

ANY WAY YOU CAN.

Because that's a nice thing for a kid to see.

Just because you're a dad, don't give up on *who you are* or *what you want* or *what you believe*.

Sure, **T** is for the *Tightrope* you'll walk every day.

But it's **U**nbelievable how you'll somehow make it all work.

And before breakfast starts featuring

Vodka, **W**hiskey or **X**anax,

I want to point something out …

For a few precious years,
your kid will think
the coolest man on the planet
is **YOU**.

Yep.

They actually will.

And finally, **Z** is for *Zen*.
(*The search for Inner Peace through tranquillity and meditation.*)

Not a fucking chance, mate.

But that's OK too.

Because one day,
when your children all leave home,
you'll be able to sit in perfect tranquillity
as much as you like.

And you know what you'll be thinking?

Gee, I miss my kids.

Aaron Blabey's life doesn't make any sense.

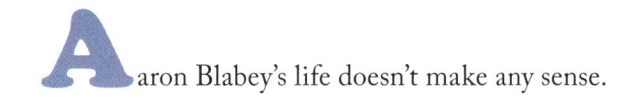

He is best known for his well-loved children's picture books for which he has won many awards including a *Children's Book Council of Australia Book of the Year Award*, a *NSW Premier's Literary Award for Children's Literature*, *Children's Peace Literature Award* and he's also been the *National Literacy Ambassador*.

But dig a little deeper and his past gets quite shady.

He spent 13 years as an actor appearing in numerous plays, TV shows and films. He was regularly cast opposite proper actors like **Hugh Jackman**, **Jacki Weaver**, **Guy Pearce**, **Bryan Brown**, **Joel Edgerton** and **Ben Mendelsohn**, all of whom were too kind to ever point out that his own acting was 'just fucking awful', as he describes it today. To his continuing bewilderment though, he did once win an *AACTA Award (AFI) for Best Actor*, a fact that cannot be adequately explained.

To complicate matters, he worked for a time as a staff writer at a major global advertising agency where he 'learned a great deal and wished for death every single day', before spending a couple of years attempting to teach 'Creative Thinking' at a prominent Sydney design college. Furthermore, he's exhibited his art in various galleries, spent some time as a grape picker, worked in a video store and – astonishingly – once modelled clothes in a glossy weekend supplement.

He lives these days in a beautiful town in the Blue Mountains with his preposterously short wife and their two gorgeous boys, where he creates books, listens to his beloved vinyl record collection through *killer* 70s speakers and celebrates loudly every fifteen minutes that one of his all-time, top-ten heroes – **Nick Cave** – recently chose to record one of his books.

All of this is true.

Oh, and he found the initial transition into fatherhood about as easy as copping a spade to the back of the head. As a result, he wrote this book.

It is his first for adults.

First published 2014 in Macmillan by Pan Macmillan Australia Pty Ltd
1 Market Street, Sydney, New South Wales, Australia, 2000

Copyright © Aaron Blabey 2014
The moral right of the author has been asserted.

All rights reserved. No part of this book may be reproduced or transmitted by any person or entity (including Google, Amazon or similar organisations), in any form or by any means, electronic or mechanical, including photocopying, recording, scanning or by any information storage and retrieval system, without prior permission in writing from the publisher.

Cataloguing-in-Publication entry is available
from the National Library of Australia
http://catalogue.nla.gov.au

Illustrations and text by Aaron Blabey
Designed by Seymour Designs and Aaron Blabey
Printed and bound in China
Reprinted 2017, 2019